# 12 DAYS OF CHRISTMAS PROJECTS

How to Make Twelve Delightful and Simple
Holiday Projects to Inspire, Enjoy and Give

by
## ROBIN MADERICH

12 Days of Christmas Projects – How to Make Twelve Delightful and Simple Holiday Projects to Inspire, Enjoy and Give

ISBN: 978-1-7345419-3-9

Available in print and e-book

Copyright © 2020 by Robin Maderich

All rights reserved. No part of this publication may be reproduced, distributed, or transmitted in any form or by any means, including photocopying, recording, or other electronic or mechanical methods, without the prior written permission of the publisher, except in the case of brief quotations embodied in critical reviews and certain other non-commercial uses permitted by copyright law. For permission requests, write to the publisher on the contact form at the website address below.

Potter Street Books – Robin Maderich Publishing
5125 Schultz Bridge Road
Zionsville, PA 18092
www.potterstreetbooks.com

Printed in the United States of America

# Disclaimer

As always, be responsible and aware. Crafters need to use care in their workspace, and for themselves and others when making crafts. Be mindful to clean up immediately after (as some materials can dry and become difficult to remove) as well as during, and the crafter should make certain not to use any materials to which the crafter or another may be sensitive or allergic. Make certain any child involved is old enough to recognize that no material or completed project is to be eaten, chewed on, or otherwise used inappropriately, and the crafter shall keep any inappropriate material away from said child.

Remember to protect the work area, covering a table with baking parchment or brown paper or newspaper. When hot glue is called for, this task must be performed only by an adult as both the glue and the glue gun nozzle are painfully hot. Take all due caution handling same. The use of a sewing needle or sewing machine is to be performed by an adult. Always follow the instructions provided by the manufacturer for all store-bought supplies. Remember, these are craft projects and this book does not offer any guarantee of their success.

This disclaimer is not exhaustive. The author and publisher cannot be held responsible for any property or medical damages caused by items you read about in this book. The information available throughout this book is for informational purposes only. By taking any information or education material from this book, you assume all risks for the material covered. You agree to indemnify, hold harmless, and defend the author and publisher from any and all claims and damages as a result of any and all of the information covered.

By taking and/or using any informational resources from this book, you agree that you will use this information in a safe and legal manner, consistent with all safety rules, and good common sense. You further agree that you will take such steps as may be reasonably necessary or required to keep any information and/or materials out of the hands of minors and untrained and/or immature individuals.

The author takes no responsibility for the misuse of any material, incautious behavior of the crafter, or any other action beyond the author's control and/or knowledge.

# DEDICATION

*This book is dedicated to the wonder of families and to the imagination of crafters and artists everywhere*

# TABLE OF CONTENTS

| | |
|---|---|
| Copyright Information | i |
| Disclaimer | ii |
| Dedication | iii |
| Introduction | 2 |
| Memory Ornaments | 3 |
| Soap Balls | 6 |
| Santa's Sack of Treats | 9 |
| Oh Christmas Tree Placeholder | 12 |
| Wooden Bead Garland | 15 |
| Mini Melt Your Heart Snowmen | 18 |
| Hand Wreath | 21 |
| Hand-Decorated Wrapping Paper | 24 |
| Holiday Coasters | 26 |
| Paper Mache Gingerbread Man | 28 |
| Paper Chain | 31 |
| Greeting, Thank You and Gift Cards | 33 |
| Hang-About Angels | 36 |
| Christmas Tree Ornament | 39 |
| Acknowledgments | 41 |

# INTRODUCTION

Christmas is a wonderful, heartwarming season, and spending time crafting with our families can make the holidays even more special, but we don't need projects that take hours and hours to complete when we are already pressed for time. The craft projects on the following pages are relatively simple and the most time necessary is often in allowing certain elements to dry, such as paper mache. If you plan ahead you can set these projects aside for drying, continue with your day, and return to the task at a later time. And despite the title of this book, there are fourteen projects inside rather than twelve, as some are remarkably quick to do and others you might choose to skip.

The projects in this book are made from objects we might otherwise recycle or throw away, articles we often have around the house, as well as materials available from your local craft store. As you make the crafts in this book, many of you will be inspired to change the project into a creation that is uniquely you. If you do, please feel free to let me know what exciting ideas you've come up with as I am always awed by the creativity displayed by crafters.

Plan ahead and stock up on what you might otherwise throw away. For example, when cardstock is called for in the supplies, you can use the cardstock already at hand—the interior of the cards you are cutting up! However, you will likely need more than what you can obtain from that source, so to avoid frustration you may wish to buy a pack of cardstock from your local craft store or office supply store. The directions are worded as if you have purchased the cardstock. You might also save and wash drinking straws from those soft drinks you purchase from a fast food restaurant. This Christmas you could gather up the wrapping paper that isn't torn beyond redemption after gifts are opened and save it for next year's projects, as well as pack up Christmas cards received that might otherwise make it into the shredder or recycling.

It is helpful to read the instructions through before starting your projects to be certain you have your supplies, and also to compare the instructions to the sample project photo at the chapter's beginning for a better understanding of each step and the end goal. Please be reminded that certain steps should be performed only by an adult. There will be reminders in the instructions, but in particular whenever hot glue is included, this part of the project is to be performed by an adult. Although I will advise to take care in the steps, the need for care is implied whether it appears or not, as the glue is HOT.

Happy crafting!

*For kits, décor and more, feel free to visit my Etsy site: tumblecreekchristmas.com*

# MEMORY ORNAMENTS

We all have old Christmas cards we hang onto (or at least I do—more than I care to admit), whether because we think they're especially pretty or they've come from someone who means a lot to us. Here is a project utilizing previously received Christmas cards (or odd leftovers that never got sent). In the example of a completed ornament on the previous page, I used a card that had a cutout along the top edge, so added glitter to the background behind the bear's heads.

## Supplies

- old Christmas cards
- white cardstock
- glue stick
- safety scissors
- pencil
- ribbon or yarn
- glitter
- hole punch
- something round to trace around (about 3" to 3.5" across, such as a large glass or coffee mug), or a large circle punch (usually cuts a circle about 3.5" across)
- gold or silver glitter pen
- Mod Podge or similar water-based sealer/decoupage glue (optional)

## Instructions

1. Gather all your supplies. Cover the area where you are planning to work.

2. Look through your Christmas cards for the ones you would like to use. Place the glass upside down on the card(s) and position it until you find the area you think would look best on your ornament. Trace around the glass with a pencil. Repeat this on each card for as many ornaments as you plan to make.

   Note:  If you would like to make a keepsake ornament for a particular card, also place the glass over the area containing the signature and/or sentiment written by the sender and cut that out as well. This will be used on the back of the ornament.

3. Cut out the circles you have traced. If you have a circle lever punch, use that instead. The card illustrations or photos will be the front of your ornament. The signature or sentiment, if you choose to use one, will be the back.

4. Next, trace the same size circles onto the white cardstock, twelve circles for each ornament you plan to make. Cut or punch them out. These will make up the interior layers of your ornament(s).

5. Take the circle made from the Christmas card, locate the top of the illustration and then take your small punch and punch a hole about a ½" from the edge. Line up your ten layer circles one at a time beneath the top circle and line up the punch in the existing hole, punching a hole in the layer beneath. Repeat with all layers. This is done to ensure the holes are all in the same place. Make sure you do the same to any signature/sentiment circle, if you are using one.

6. With your glue stick, place an even coat of glue on a circle, making certain not to miss the edges. Line up the next blank layer and press firmly into place. Repeat until you have all layers glued together. Place an even coat of glue on the last layer and line up your card/ornament front and press firmly into place. If you are making a keepsake ornament, place an even coat of glue on the back side of your ornament and line up the signature sentiment facing out and press firmly into place.

7. Once your ornaments have dried, sprinkle glitter onto a paper plate, a piece of foil, or the baking parchment. Run the glue stick around the outer edge of your ornament and roll the ornaments edgewise through the glitter. Lay the ornament(s) aside in a clean space to dry once again.

8. On the blank backs of the ornament(s), write a fun holiday sentiment or personalize with the name of someone you plan to give the ornament to as a gift for their own tree.

9. If desired, put a light coat of acrylic sealer over each ornament and allow the sealer to dry.

10. Cut your yarn or ribbon into lengths about twelve 15" long. Cut as many lengths as you need so you have one for each ornament you've made. Slip the ribbon or yarn through the hole at the top of each ornament and tie a knot about 3" above the ornament, then tie the remaining length into a bow.

11. Your ornaments are ready to hang!

# SOAP BALLS

This is a fun project for little hands, but be certain those little hands don't go into those little mouths. Soap doesn't taste good and should never be eaten. Also, the grating of soap with a cheese grater **must** be performed by an ADULT, as the grater is sharp. When completed, the soap balls are fun to use and to give as gifts. Four ounces of grated soap will make approximately three 2" soap balls.

## Supplies

- unscented, child safe soap
- clean cheese grater
- baking parchment
- distilled water
- mixing bowl
- small holiday treat bags or cling film
- hole punch
- ribbon
- white cardstock
- safety scissors
- soap dye (optional)

## Instructions

1. Purchase several bars of mild, unscented soap. ADULTS grate the bars as you would cheese onto a sheet of baking parchment. Once grated, fold the parchment paper and pour the grated soap along the fold into the mixing bowl. Tap the bowl to make sure the shredded soap settles.

2. Pour one tablespoon of distilled water into the grated soap for every four ounces of soap grated. It is important to use distilled water to keep out any tap water impurities.

3. If desired, you may add soap dye and/or body glitter obtained from your local craft store. Be sure to follow manufacturer's instructions.

4. Work grated soap and water with your hands until it has the consistency of soft clay.

5. When your soap is the correct consistency, have fun rolling the soap into balls on your palms (about 2" across are a good size). You may need to squeeze as well as roll to make certain the soap balls hold their shape. Place the balls on parchment paper to dry.

6. Once the soap balls are set (holding together and no longer feeling wet), either place each soap ball individually into small holiday treat bags or wrap with cling film. Twist the bag or cling film closed, leaving enough material to wrap a ribbon around.

7. Cut small squares from your cardstock. Write something jolly on the squares and also identify the contents of the bags or cling film as soap (just to make sure no one mistakes them for something other than what they are—you can use words such as Soap Balls –Joy for your Hands). Punch holes in the squares at the upper left corner.

8. Attach the squares to each wrapped ball of soap with a piece of ribbon. They are now ready to place into a container in the bathroom as guest soaps or give to friends as gifts.

# SANTA'S GIFT BAG

**W**hat could be more enjoyable than a bag full of goodies? You make the sack and afterward you can fill with your own choice of wrapped candies or candy canes, individually wrapped cookies, or twenty-four folded squares on which you've written fun things to do over the holiday season. One folded paper could be pulled out per day and the instructions within followed, making it a treasure hunt-style advent calendar. The example on the previous page shows an embellishment of fake greenery, which is optional. If you have decided to make a bag for each child at a dinner or party, you can also leave off the jingle bell and merely replace with a wider piece of ribbon hot glued into place.

## Supplies

- one 9 oz. paper cup for each sack you plan to make
- brown felt
- hot glue gun
- safety scissors
- cardstock
- polyester stuffing or shredded paper
- ribbon
- paper clips
- jingle bell and fake greenery (optional)

## Instructions

1. Gather your supplies. Cover the area where you are going to be working.

2. Trace a circle onto your cardstock, using the top of the cup. Cut out the circle and center and glue it to the bottom of the cup using hot glue (ADULTS only). Follow the manufacturer's instructions for use of the hot glue gun.

3. Using the top of the cup, trace a circle onto the felt and cut it out. Hot glue the circle of felt over the cardstock you have previously glued to the cup.

4. Cut a rectangle from the felt, 5" high and 12" long. Form a 5" high cylinder from the rectangle. Make sure the cylinder is wide enough to slip loosely over the cup. When you have made sure it will fit, paper clip the top and bottom of the rectangle to hold the piece together. Using the hot glue gun, glue the overlap of felt to the felt beneath and carefully (avoiding, as always, touching the hot glue) press the two pieces together. Let cool.

5. Slide the felt cylinder over the cup. Use the hot glue gun to glue the bottom of the cylinder to the felt and cardstock circle. Let cool.

6. Push the fiber stuffing or shredded paper down between the cup and the felt to create a firm bulge in the sack.

7. Run hot glue around the upper edge of the cup. Press the felt against the glue to form the mouth of the sack. Let cool.

8. Tie a ribbon around the outside of the sack. Add embellishment such as a jingle bell and/or greenery as desired. Fluff out the top of the sack.

9. Your project is now ready to fill with wrapped goodies!

# OH CHRISTMAS TREE PLACEHOLDER

**F**amilies gather around the holidays, and sometimes we are a large crowd. A fun way to set the table and make sure everyone knows where they are sitting is to use placeholders with the family member or friend's name on them.

## Supplies

- Styrofoam cones, about 3" tall
- instant paper mache
- green or white paint
- red or gold ribbon, 1/8" wide
- Sharpie or similar marker
- safety scissors
- Mod Podge or similar water-based sealer/decoupage glue and applicator
- cardstock or gold foil paper (or alternatively, small wooden stars from the craft store)
- hole punch (to make gold foil or other color dots)
- hot glue gun

## Instructions

1. First, gather all your supplies and prepare your work space. Decide how many placeholders you will need and make certain you have enough material to make them.

2. Use a pencil to make a shallow indentation across the bottom of each Styrofoam cone, and a deeper one straight down into the very top.

3. Prepare your instant paper mache according to product directions (or make paper mache using strips of newspaper and flour and water solution). Thinly and evenly coat each Styrofoam cone with paper mache except the bottom surface. Make sure you leave the hole in the top open. Stand the cones up to completely dry. The drying process may take a day or two, so plan accordingly.

    Note: You can store any leftover prepared instant paper mache in a sealed sandwich bag for a few days to use on other projects.

4. Once the paper mache has dried, paint the cones green or white. Allow the cones to dry.

5. When dry, apply a water-based urethane or acrylic sealer with a brush or sponge applicator to the cones.

6. Cut two star shapes from white cardstock or gold foil paper. Use glue (or a glue stick) to adhere the two stars together to make them sturdier (if using gold foil paper, the gold sides should be facing outward).

7. If you have decided to use wooden stars (shown in the example), paint the stars and set aside to dry.

8. After the sealed cones have dried, press the end of your ribbon into the indentation at the bottom of the cone and (ADULTS) adhere with a small bit of hot glue. When the glue is cool, set the cone upright and wrap the ribbon diagonally around the cone until you reach the top. Cut the ribbon, leaving a slight excess. Put a small dab of hot glue into the hole at the top of the cone and press the excess ribbon into the hole with a toothpick (rather than fingers).

9. Using your Sharpie or other pen, write the name of a guest on each star.

10. Place a further dab of hot glue into the indentation at the top and position the star over the hole, pressing the edge lightly into the hot glue. Let cool.

11. Set your placeholders on your table.

# WOODEN BEAD GARLAND

Making this garland is **a** delightful project that can be adjusted to your length of choice, whether to wrap around a small potted plant, across a window, or long enough to decorate your Christmas tree. You will note in the example that I chose my paint colors to coordinate with the wrapping paper I picked, painting the smallest beads basil green and apple red in a repeated pattern and the medium sized beads in white, blue and pink, alternating every third section. I purchased the wooden beads at the craft store in a package that contained three sizes, the largest being approximately one inch.

## Supplies

- acrylic paint (your choice of color) and medium sized artist's paintbrush
- wooden beads
- old wrapping paper
- plastic drinking straw(s) – (hint: wash the ones you may have received in a soft drink and save for projects like these!)
- colored cotton string (available in craft stores)
- Mod Podge or similar sealer and sponge applicator (optional)
- safety scissors
- 1 ½" inch circle paper punch (optional)
- glue stick

## Instructions

1. Prepare your workspace and gather your materials.

2. Choose your wrapping paper and paint colors.

3. Cut the plastic drinking straw into lengths of approximately one inch.

4. Decide on your garland length and place your beads and cut straw pieces into a pattern. Once you have done so, remove the beads by size and set aside.

   Note: You may wish to hold out enough beads for the next project.

5. Cut the chosen wrapping paper into 1.5" circles (or use the paper punch), with two circles for each 1" wooden bead you plan to use.

6. Coat the underside of a wrapping paper circle with the glue from the glue stick. Press the center of the wooden bead (not the ends with the holes) into the center of the wrapping paper circle. Push the paper firmly onto the bead, making sure the edges are pressed down. Repeat for the other side of the bead. If any paper covers the holes, press into the hole with a toothpick.

7. Repeat the process for all the large beads you plan to use. Set these wrapped beads aside.

8. Cut the chosen wrapping paper into strips 1¼" wide by 2" long. Coat the underside of a strip with glue from the glue stick. Place the cut drinking straw at one end of the underside of the paper and roll the paper around the straw. Using a pencil, tuck the overlap at each end into the interior. Repeat as necessary and set the straw "beads" aside.

9. Paint the remainder of the wooden beads the colors you have chosen following the pattern you have decided upon and let dry. The most stress-free way to do so, is to paint one half of the bead and set it down on a flat, protected surface to dry (hole side down), then paint the other half and let it dry (hole side down).

10. If desired, coat the beads with Mod Podge or similar sealer using a sponge applicator and let dry.

11. Unwind a length of string and push the end through the first bead in your pattern. Continue to push the string through the beads to create your chosen pattern, unwinding more string as needed. When you reach the last bead, tie a knot in the end of the string large enough that it will not be pulled back through the beads. Cut the string at the beginning of your garland and knot, making sure that you leave enough slack in the length of the garland so it wraps properly around your tree and is not too tight.

12. Your garland is ready to be hung. Do not hang the garland where it might be accessible to small children or pets.

# Mini Melt Your Heart Snowmen

This little snowman is made almost entirely from purchased supplies, but is worth it, as he looks adorable hanging from a tree, a wreath, or adorning a gift. As mentioned above, you hopefully were able to set aside several sets of the three different-sized wooden beads for this project.

## Supplies

- acrylic paint – white, orange, black, red
- small paint brush
- three wooden beads of graduated sizes
- small paperclip
- ribbon
- small wooden heart(s)
- small jingle bell(s)
- narrow gauge brown crafting or jewelry wire
- hot glue gun
- toothpicks
- white school glue
- masking tape

## Instructions

1. Gather your supplies and prepare your workspace.

2. Insert two toothpicks through the smallest wood bead. Apply white school glue around the hole at the top of the middle sized wood bead. Push the toothpicks into the middle sized wood bead and press the smallest wood bead down into the glue. Apply white school glue around the hole at the top of the largest bead. While holding the small and middle-sized beads, push the toothpicks into the largest bead, pressing the middle sized bead into the glue. You should be able to set your three glued beads upright to dry, with the toothpicks still in place holding them together.

3. ADULTS: Measure a 7" length of wire and cut. Take each end and fold until they meet in the middle. Wrap a bit of masking tape around the cut ends and the wire where they meet, securing them in place. Holding the cut ends and tape securely between thumb and finger of one hand, twist each loop, one at a time, until the entire "arm" is twisted but leaving a small circle of wire at the end.

4. Paint a small wooden heart with red paint and let dry.

5. When the glue is dried on your snowman, gently wiggle and remove the toothpicks. Paint the snowmen white. Set aside to dry.

6. ADULTS: Carefully using the hot glue gun according to manufacturer's instructions, apply a dab of hot glue to the snowman's "neck" which is formed between the small and medium sized beads. Press the masking tape portion of the arms into the hot glue and let cool.

7. Cut ribbon to a 6" length. Wrap around the snowman's neck. Drape an end over the front of the snowman and over the back. Tack in place with a dab of hot glue.

8. Hot glue the painted, dry heart to the area where the largest and middle sized beads meet. Let cool.

9. Bend the wire arms so the circle "hands" are clutching the heart.

10. Dab the end of a toothpick into the orange paint and place the drop gently on the face area where the nose should be. Dab the opposite end of the toothpick into the black paint and place the drop gently onto the face area where one of the eyes should be. Repeat for the other. Let dry.

11. Straighten the longer end of the paper clip. Leave the other end curved and slip the jingle bell onto it. Squeeze the curve to close it as much as possible. Slide the straight end up through the snowman from the bottom until it sticks out the top.

12. Using the handle of the artist's paintbrush for leverage, curve the straight edge until the tip is near the hole at the top of the snowman's head. Wriggle the end into the hole and squeeze slightly. Insert a ribbon into the hanger you've made and your snowman is ready to adorn your tree, wreath or gift.

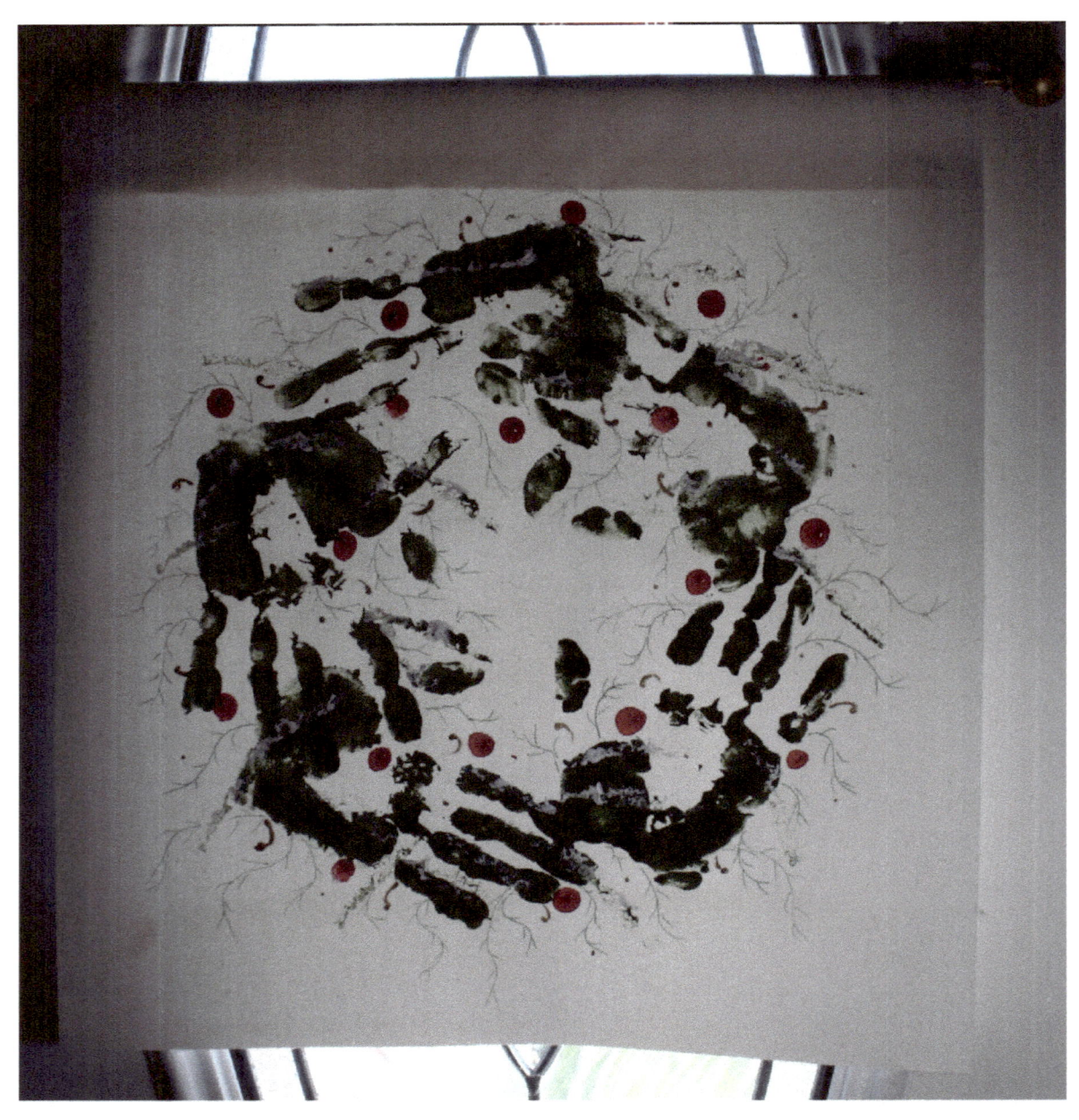

# HAND WREATH

Many years ago when my children were little and in school, my youngest son brought home an adorable project he and his classmates had each made. With some additions, I am sharing this project with you because I thought (and still do) that it was precious and imaginative and a wonderful keepsake. Since my children are all grown, I have used my own hands to make the example on the previous page.

## Supplies

- one yard bleached or unbleached muslin or a 16" x 20" heavy paper or canvas sheet from an artist's pad
- two 1" wood ball finials/dowel caps (per wreath)
- three 3/8" wooden craft dowels, 12" long (to fit into the finials)
- red and green finger paint
- white and gold acrylic paints
- thin and medium art paint brush
- hot glue gun or needle and thread
- green watercolor or fabric makers
- kitchen sponge
- masking tape
- paper towels
- ribbon or yarn

## Instructions

1. Prepare your workspace and gather your materials. Place newspaper beneath the entire area of the muslin or paper when you are ready to begin painting, as the paint may leak through.

2. Paint 6" at one end of two dowels and the entirety of the finials with gold paint. Let dry. Overlap the two dowels so they have an overall length of approximately 18" and (ADULT) hot glue the dowels together at that point. Line up the third dowel parallel and centered over the connected area of the two painted dowels and carefully hot glue the third dowel to the two painted dowels. When cool, wrap the dowels with masking tape. Make certain not to wrap masking tape over the painted portions.

3. Cut your muslin into a rectangle 18" wide by 24" long.

4. Fold over an inch of fabric at the right and left sides. Either sew the fabric in place with a simple stitch, or carefully use hot glue. If gluing, allow the glue to cool. If using paper, skip this step.

5. Fold over an inch of fabric at the bottom. Either sew the fabric in place with a simple stitch, or glue with hot glue and allow the glue to dry. If using paper, skip this step.
6. Fold over 2.5" inches of fabric at the top. Either sew the fabric in place with a simple stitch or glue with hot glue and allow the glue to cool. Make sure you leave 1.5" of open space for insertion of the dowels later. If using paper, skip to the next step.

7. Fold over without creasing 2.5" of paper from the top. Glue the edge down to the back of the paper, leaving room for the dowels to be inserted later.

8. Using an 8" or 9" paper plate and a pencil, trace a circle centered in each square of muslin or paper your have prepared. Set the plate aside.

9. Place a small amount of green finger paint onto the paper plate and spread thinly. Have your child press his or her hand into the paint so paint lightly covers the palm and underside of fingers.

10. Have your child press his or her hand onto the muslin or paper, following the penciled circle (see example for positioning). Repeat as necessary (including applying more paint to your child's hand) until a circle of handprints is completed. Clean up with paper towels and have your child wash the paint from his or her hands.

11. Pour a small amount of red finger paint into a clear spot on the paper plate. Have your child press a forefinger into the red paint and press the tip of his or her forefinger onto the fabric in various places (see example). Clean up with paper towels and have your child wash the paint from his or her hands. Allow the wreath to dry.

12. Cut off a half inch from a kitchen sponge. Dip the edge (not the whole piece) into a bit of white paint and lightly press onto the "wreath" for highlights. With a green marker, and following the direction of the hands, make wispy lines to represent evergreen branches, extending away from the hands toward the outside edge of the paper/muslin and toward the center of the wreath. With gold paint or marker, make some curlicues. See example for illustration. Allow the wreath to dry again.

13. When dry, push the dowels through the opening at the top. Glue the finials onto the exposed ends of the dowels.

14. Cut a length of ribbon 30" long. Tie one end of the ribbon to the dowel on the left side of your wreath. Tie the other end of the ribbon to the dowel on the right side or your wreath. The wreath is ready to display.

# Hand-Decorated Wrapping Paper

What grandparent, family member or special friend wouldn't love to receive a gift wrapped in hand-decorated wrapping paper? This is a perfect project for the kids, but even adults can have fun decorating their own wrapping paper. It is hard these days to get your hands on brown paper bags, although if you only plan to wrap small gifts with the hand-decorated paper, you could purchase a package of lunch bags from the grocery store. If not, purchase a roll of butcher paper or a roll of brown kraft paper from a craft store. This project's instructions will proceed as if you are using a roll, but the same steps would be used for bags from which you would remove the bottoms once the bag has been cut at one seam, and then lay the paper flat on your workspace.

## Supplies

- brown bags or roll of butcher paper or kraft paper
- finger paint and/or crayons and/or colored markers and/or watercolor paints
- rubber stamps and ink pads (optional)
- glitter pens or colored markers

## Instructions

1. Prepare your workspace. Gather your supplies.

2. Spread your paper across your workspace and measure out three feet in length. Cut the paper to length. If necessary, place an object at each corner to keep the paper flat (full soup cans are a good choice).

3. Prepare for use whatever you have chosen to decorate the paper, whether paints, crayons, rubber stamps and ink and start having fun applying same to the paper. Children can make handprints across the paper using finger paint. The choice and execution of ideas are totally yours.

4. If using paints or ink, allow your work to dry.

5. Write holiday sentiments in some of the blank spaces with the glitter pens.

6. When you are finished, roll your unique wrapping paper back up and set aside for use when wrapping your gifts later on.

# HOLIDAY COASTERS

These coasters will likely only last one season, but they will be fun to create and use, and your kids can proudly point out that they have made them. Once again, we will be recycling old Christmas cards or scraps of wrapping paper. Being a cat lover (an animal lover in general, actually) I adore the cat coaster above.

## Supplies

- old wrapping paper (from the rolls that were never quite finished)
- old Christmas cards
- white cardstock
- glue stick
- Mod Podge or similar water-based sealer/decoupage glue and sponge applicator
- safety scissors
- ruler or round glass or 3.5" circle or square lever punch
- cork backing (optional)

## Instructions

1. Measure and mark a 3.5" square on white cardstock, or trace a 3.5" diameter circle. Repeat twelve times and cut out all.

2. Next mark the same size square or circle onto the segment of the Christmas card(s) or wrapping paper you wish to use as the top for the coaster.

3. With your glue stick, place an even coat of glue over the first cardstock layer of your coaster. Line up the next layer and press firmly into place. Repeat until you have glued and firmly pressed all of your layers together. Finish by adding the cut-out from your Christmas card or wrapping paper.

4. When the coaster layers are dry, you may desire to coat the finished coaster with Mod Podge or whatever sealer you have chosen. Let the first side dry before coating the other side and the edges, so that your piece does not stick to the surface where it has been left to dry.

    Note: You may also wish to utilize the pre-cut corkboard available for coasters at your craft store. If you choose to do so, either cut the corkboard to the size of your coaster or upsize your cardstock and Christmas card/wrapping paper cutout to match the size of the corkboard. When using corkboard, you may reduce the number of cardstock layers to six. Once the cardstock and top layer are all adhered, glue your creation with white school glue to the corkboard.

5. Once the coating has completely dried, your coasters are ready to be used.

# Paper Mache Gingerbread Man

Gingerbread houses and gingerbread men are iconic when it comes to the holidays. This gingerbread man is made from paper mache and is meant to be hung on your tree as a jolly reminder of the season. I have made mine the thickness of my particular cookie cutter, making for a hefty (although fairly lightweight) decoration. You may make yours as thin as an actual cookie, or anywhere in between. Just remember that the thicker the paper mache, the longer the dry time. I also used strips of fabric for his scarf and as a hanger to add to the primitive style.

This project doesn't have to be limited to a gingerbread man, as you can use other cookie cutters such as stars and Christmas trees, or whatever you have that will work. If you don't have cookie cutters, you can roll or press the paper mache flat and cut out the paper mache around paper stencils.

## Supplies

- plastic sandwich bag
- gingerbread man cookie cutter
- instant paper mache
- baking parchment
- Mod Podge or similar sealer/decoupage glue and sponge applicator
- strips of fabric, ribbon or yarn
- safety scissors
- plastic drinking straw
- sand paper or sanding sponge
- brown, black and white acrylic paint and paint brush
- white school glue and glitter (optional)
- adhesive pearls available at your craft store (optional)

## Instructions

1. Gather your ingredients and prepare your work space.

2. Prepare a small quantity of instant paper mache according to manufacturer's directions. (Hint: I prepare mine in a plastic sandwich bag for small jobs, where it can be mixed and also stored for a time.)

3. Place your cookie cutter onto a square of baking parchment cut to exceed the size of the cutter by about 2" on all sides.

4. Using a little at a time, press the paper mache into the cookie cutter, making sure it is pushed to the edges. Add more bit by bit until you have filled the cookie cutter (or to whatever level you wish).

5. Gently push one limb at a time and the head as you carefully remove the cookie cutter. This make take several times around from limb to limb to head to limb to limb while you work the cutter up, since you don't want to yank it all at once as your paper mache will become misshapen or rip apart. However, if this does happen, you only have to repeat step 4 using the same paper mache.

6. Press your plastic straw into the upper center of the head and turn to remove a section of paper mache. This hole will later house the ribbon for hanging.

7. Press two tiny balls of paper mache onto the body for "buttons" or, in the alternative, apply adhesive pearls as buttons once you have painted your ornament.

8. Set the gingerbread man aside to dry on the piece of baking parchment. Depending on the thickness, this may take up to several days, so plan accordingly.

9. Once dry, lightly sand your creations to remove rough edges and then paint with brown paint. Paint the buttons black (or whatever color you choose), or apply the adhesive pearls. Although the pearls have an adhesive back, I would recommend an additional dab of glue to make sure they stick to the surface of your gingerbread man.

10. When the paint has dried, you may give the color more depth by "antiquing" it. Mix a few drops of black paint with water or floating medium and coat the ornament. Wipe down while still wet with a paper towel to remove any excess. The darker color will fill cracks and indentations to give it a more "antiqued" look. Let dry.

11. To create a "piped" look, outline the gingerbread man by squeezing white school glue from the bottle to follow the shape of your ornament. Sprinkle glitter on the glue while wet. Let everything dry.

12. Coat the ornament(s) with Mod Podge or other acrylic sealer. Allow to dry again.

13. Cut an 8" strip of fabric (or ribbon or yarn) and tie around the neck of your gingerbread man like a scarf. Cut a 12" strip of fabric (or ribbon or yarn) and slip through the hole in the head and tie for hanging.

# Paper Chains

Paper chains are nostalgic for a lot of us. As children, we made them from construction paper in school and at home, draping them everywhere. This project is an updated version. In the example, I made mine using both sides of leftover double sided wrapping paper, but you can choose two different papers with complimentary or contrasting colors. To save time, you could make a really colorful chain by gathering up whatever old cards you haven't used yet and cutting strips from them instead of the two-step process below.

## Supplies

- old wrapping paper
- cardstock
- glue stick
- ruler
- safety scissors or (ADULTS) a paper trimmer, if you have one

## Instructions

1. Gather your supplies and prepare your workspace.

2. Pick out the wrapping paper(s) you plan to use. Cut pieces 8.5" wide by 11" long. Coat the back of the paper and press onto a piece of 8.5" x 11" cardstock and let dry. Make sure your design runs left to right across the width of the paper, not lengthwise.

3. Using a ruler, mark the paper at 6.5" at the top, middle and bottom. Draw a line through your marks and either cut with scissors or use a paper trimmer.

4. Turn the glued cardstock and paper over. Mark from top to bottom on the left and right every ¾". Draw a line across from one side to the other for each set of marks and cut with scissors or use a paper trimmer.

5. Repeat steps 2 through 4 as needed, depending on how many links you will need for your chain.

6. Turn the glue stick so glue is above the rim. Press the end of a strip onto the glue and slide across, covering a section of about ¾". Gently roll the strip into a circle and press the glued area onto the opposite end of the strip to create a circle.

7. Repeat the same with the next strip, but before you press the glued end to the opposite end, slid the unglued end through the circle you just made. Press the glued end to the opposite end of the circle you are creating to form linked circles.

8. Proceed with the remainder of your strips until you have no more left. Your paper chain is now ready to hang. (As stated above, you can make the whole chain using leftover cards for a colorful effect without the step of gluing paper to cardstock.)

# Greeting, Thank You Cards and Gift Tags

These cards and gift tags are easy to make. The cards are designed to fit into envelopes readily available at your grocery or office supply store. The gift tags will be a fun addition to packaged gifts, gift bags, or cookie tins.

## Supplies

- white cardstock
- hole punch
- ribbon
- gold foil paper
- old wrapping paper
- white glitter
- safety scissors
- glue stick
- ruler
- other small paper punches, such as stars or snowflakes (optional)

## Instructions

1. Prepare your work area. Gather your supplies.

2. For gifts cards: Measure and mark 2" high by 4" wide rectangles the length of a sheet of card stock. Cut out the rectangles. Fold the rectangles in half, so that they make 2" x 2" squares.

3. Cut 2" x 2" squares of wrapping paper. Using your glue stick, glue the wrapping paper onto the cardstock front (making sure the cardstock fold is on the left).

4. Punch a hole in the upper left corner of each card.

5. Punch holes or other shapes in the gold foil paper. Using a glue stick, glue the gold dots or shapes onto the wrapping paper. You can also punch holes or shapes into a variety of papers and use them in the same way. (I have found the easiest way to glue them on is to touch the top of the dot/shape with your fingertip so it clings to your skin, then rub the dot/shape lightly over the glue stick and press down onto the gift tag. If glue builds up on your fingertip, wash your finger and thoroughly dry before continuing.)

6. Insert a 6" length of ribbon through the hole on each card and tie the ribbon ends into a small knot.

7. For greeting cards: Measure and mark an 8.5" x 6.25" rectangle and cut. Fold the rectangle in half so it forms a card 4.25" wide by 6.25" tall.

8. Choose your wrapping paper and cut a rectangle 4.5" wide by 6.25" tall. Coat the underside with glue from the glue stick, line up with the card front and press into place, folding the excess over onto the back to give a nice, finished look.

9. Cut out various shapes from cardstock (the example shows a Christmas tree and hole-punched snowflakes and a star) and glue into place. You may wish to cut out a large snowflake or an element from an old Christmas card, or highlight illustrations on the paper with glitter. The choice of decoration is limitless and yours!

10. Write a nice sentiment inside, sign and mail in a purchased envelope.

11. For thank you cards: Measure and mark a 7" by 5" rectangle and cut. Fold the rectangle in half so it forms a card 3.5" wide and 5" tall.

12. Choose your wrapping paper and cut a rectangle 3.75" wide and 5" tall. Coat the underside with glue from the glue stick, line up with the card front and press into place, folding the excess over onto the back to give a nice, finished look.

13. If you have a computer and printer, print out onto cardstock the words Thank You, Please Come for Party, or whatever you need to, making sure the space the words take up is no wider than 2.75" and no higher than 4". Cut out the rectangle with its printed words, edge with gold or silver paint or marker and glue onto the card. If you don't have a computer, you can write what you wish by hand.

14. Write a note or party details inside and mail out in a purchased envelope.

# HANG–ABOUT ANGEL

**A**ngels in our homes are symbols of peace and joy. This simple angel is constructed using cardstock and wrapping paper, and makes an adorable decoration on your tree, at a window, on a wreath or hanging from a doorknob. They could also be used as placeholders or gift tags.

## Supplies

- ✓ cardstock
- ✓ old wrapping paper
- ✓ glue stick
- ✓ hole punch
- ✓ ribbon
- ✓ safety scissors
- ✓ ruler
- ✓ pencil
- ✓ red marker or acrylic paint and paint brush, or red cardstock or construction paper

## Instructions

1. Gather your supplies and prepare your workspace. Choose the wrapping paper you plan to use. It can be one style for all four angels or a different piece for each one.

2. Cut a sheet of 8.5" x 11" cardstock into four same-sized pieces. Repeat this on nine more sheets.

3. At the top (short side) of one of the smaller rectangles you have made, trace an approximately 1.5" circle. The top of a medication bottle is usually about that size.

4. Make a dot with the pencil in the center of the circle. Line up your ruler from the dot to the bottom right edge of the cardstock. Draw a line. Line up your ruler from the center of the circle to the bottom left edge of the cardstock. Draw a line.

5. Cut out the shape. Using this shape as a stencil, trace and cut the same shape into all the cardstock rectangles.

6. Punch a hole centered and about a ½" from the edge of the circle top of your stencil. One at a time, line up the other cut-outs beneath the stencil and line up the punch in the existing hole, punching a hole in the cut-out beneath. Repeat with all layers. This is done to ensure the holes are all in the same place.

7. Using your glue stick, place an even coat of glue on the stencil cut-out, making certain not to miss the edges. Line up the next blank layer and press firmly into place. Repeat until you have ten layers glued together. Repeat this process three more times. You will have four blank angels at this point.

8. Cut a rectangle of wrapping paper slightly larger than the angel. Place the wrapping paper face down. Placing an angel on the paper, trace around the angel with the pencil, making certain you also mark the hole. Cut out the shape from the wrapping paper and punch out the hole. Repeat. Do the same again for each angel.

9. Using the glue stick, line up and glue the wrapping paper right side out to the front of your angel, smoothing and pressing firmly into place. Repeat for the back side.

10. Cut out a heart shape from the cardstock, approximately 1.5" in size. Using this cut-out as a stencil, trace and cut out eleven more hearts.

11. Glue three heart shape layers together and repeat three more times so that you have four hearts.

12. Color the front of each heart red with your marker or paint and set aside to dry. If you have cut the hearts from red cardstock, skip this step.

13. Glue a heart to the front of each angel about 2.5" down from the top.

14. Cut a 7" length of ribbon and tie around the neck area. You may wish to add a dot of glue to keep the ribbon in place.

15. Fold a sheet of 8.5" x 11" white cardstock in half lengthwise. Trace four 2.5" circles on the cardstock, making sure one edge of each circle slightly overlaps the fold. With the paper still folded, cut out the circles, leaving them attached at the fold.

16. Open the cut circles so that you have four sets of "wings". Glue a set of wings to the back of each angel.

17. Cut a 12" length of ribbon for each angel, loop through the hole in the head and tie for hanging.

# CHRISTMAS TREE ORNAMENT

These ornaments are super easy and super quick to make. Hang them on the tree, from a wreath, or use as gift tags or placeholders at your table.

## Supplies

- green cardstock
- glue stick
- safety scissors
- hole punch
- gold foil paper
- ribbon, yarn or string
- one sheet of copy paper
- pencil
- ruler

## Instructions

1. Prepare your workspace and gather your supplies.

2. Mark a rectangle on the copy paper 3.5" wide and 5" tall. Fold the rectangle in half lengthwise. Trace a line from the top of the fold to the opposite bottom corner. Cut along the line and open up the paper. This will be the template for your tree.

3. Using your template, trace ten triangle "trees" and cut them out. Punch a hole about ¾" from the top of one, then line up the others one at a time beneath and punch a corresponding hole in each layer.

    Note: Repeat Step 3 as necessary for as many Christmas tree ornaments as you plan to make.

4. Using your glue stick, place an even coat of glue on your first layer, making certain not to miss the edges. Line up the next blank layer and press firmly into place. Repeat until you have glued all ten layers together.

5. Punch out gold dots from the gold foil paper with your punch. Glue to your tree either randomly, or like a string of garland, or in whatever pattern suits you. Decorate both sides of the Christmas tree ornament.

6. Cut a 15" length of ribbon. Insert both ends through the hole at the top of your tree and tie a bow.

7. Your Christmas tree ornament is ready to hang from the tree, a wreath, or use as a gift tag or placeholder.

## Acknowledgement

First and foremost, I would like to thank my family for their support and enthusiasm.

I would also like to thank all the wonderful greeting card and wrapping paper designers for providing such an abundance of choices when searching through old cards and paper for the crafts in this book. I do not think I would have been as inspired to make this book if not for them.

Thank you to the writing group members for their encouragement in all my endeavors. We are a likeminded, persistent sisterhood and I hope we always shall be.

And thank you to my mother, who made Christmas such a special time so long ago. That magic will never leave me.

I truly hope you—as readers and crafters, parents and teachers—have enjoyed this how-to book. Look for future volumes with simple (or not so simple) craft ideas. If you have any questions, please feel free to contact me through my website, robinmaderichwrites.com.

You may also wish to have a look at my Etsy site for available Christmas décor and greeting card kits at: **www.tumblecreekchristmas.com**

Also available from Robin Maderich ~

    **H is for Home** – a fully illustrated Family Read-Aloud children's Christmas ABC book including crafts and conversation starters – available in hard cover, paperback and e-book

    Coming soon ~ **Wreaths: Celebrating Midwinter**

For the adult reader:

    **Hurry Home for Christmas** – Book I in the Connor Falls Christmas Romance Series

    **Winter Light** – a Connor Falls Christmas novella

    Coming soon: **A Connor Falls Christmas Collection** – three heartwarming, seasonal novellas in one volume